450

THE CHOIR VAULTS OF
BEAUVAIS CATHEDRAL,
WHICH WERE THE WORLD'S
TALLEST, COLLAPSED IN
1284

'WELL NOBODY IS PERFECT'

Jerry Krüger

A HISTORY OF ARCHITECTURE ON THE DISPARATIVE METHOD

With Apologies to Sir Banister Fletcher

(All Eighteen Editions)

Written and Illustrated by

Forrest Wilson

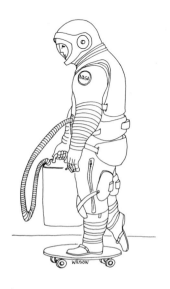

VNR *Van Nostrand Reinhold Company*
New York Cincinnati Toronto London Melbourne

For Paul, Robert, Jonathan and Betty

Van Nostrand Reinhold Company Regional Offices: New York, Cincinnati, Chicago, Millbrae, Dallas
Van Nostrand Reinhold Company International Offices: London, Toronto, Melbourne

Library of Congress Catalog Card Number 74-11594
ISBN 0-442-29544-8

Published by Van Nostrand Reinhold Company
A Division of Litton Educational Publishing, Inc.
450 West 33rd Street, New York, N. Y. 10001

16 15 14 13 12 11 10 9 8 7 6 5 4 3 2 1

Thanks is extended to Progressive Architecture for permission to publish drawings and text from "Some Modest Proposals for the Redesign of Man" appearing in 1966 and to Mr. David Travers of Arts and Architecture for permission to re-publish "The Nodule On The Module and The Art of War," which appeared in Arts and Architecture, 1964, 1965.

Library of Congress Cataloging in Publication Data

Wilson, Forrest, 1918-
    A history of architecture on the disparative method.

    1. Architecture--History-- Anecdotes, facetiae, satire, etc.   I. Title.
NA2599.W54   720'.9   74-11594
ISBN 0-442-29544-8

CONTENTS

PREFACE

This guide to the technique of reading between the lines of nonsensical texts is dedicated to lively young minds oppressed by dead scholarship.

Histories of architecture seem invariably to be compiled by tired historians who have painstakenly gleaned their ideas from the leavings of all that made life and building interesting during the period described.

This is a method of self-defense to be used against historians who learnedly describe the intentions of past builders and the harmonious proportions of their buildings which in reality were never seen in their entirety by either their builders or their users. Open city space is a modern phenomenon. The buildings of antiquity, the Middle Ages, and the Renaissance were huddled behind protective walls and could not afford such luxuries. We cannot blame historians for taking liberty with the truth. The truth is, after all, only the last resort of men without imagination. But we can condemn them for being so deadly dull. Architecture is the mother of the arts, but she is also a remarkably freehearted lady with all the zest that that implies.

As historians roll out the barrel vault, learnedly discuss the punitive pendentive and the squeaking squinch, and document their insights with countless footloose footnotes of one Ph.D. clarifying the assumptions, usually erroneous and always trivial, of some previous Ph.D., the result is invariably a severe pain in the reader's groin vault. Learned men argue about the number of angels that could dance on the head of a pin and entirely ignore the fact that it would have been a ridiculous and painful dance floor.

We know from histories other than those of architecture that the gleesome fleasome medieval mason carved obscene sculptures on lofty cathedral capitals to plague his client, the stilted churchman, who was too timid to climb the scaffolding. We know that Renaissance buildings were invented as a public-relations gimmick by merchant princes to assert their importance in a conflict with feudal nobility.

Unfortunately, this countinghouse nobility was not content to merely adopt another building style and let it go at that. The artists and architects became the real victims of the hoax, for they took themselves seriously. As a consequence, they misinterpreted the simple, natural act of design, common to all men, as a divine act of which only they were capable. We might have survived even this perversion, for it is obvious that Renaissance artists and their clients were foolish men, but historians have insisted upon taking them at their own evaluation and spawned a lot of nonsense.

This does not mean that some buildings of the past were not magnificent. Some of them were, but many were silly and fell down. The beauty of architecture, like the beauty of people, is best understood in contrast to its faults. A biography of a totally virtuous person is probably a lie and always a bore.

Things do not have to be this way. Learning can be mixed with humor, design with satisfaction, and scholarship with the joy of learning, although it is doubtful that this will often occur in most established universities.

This guide to the technique of daydreaming over boring texts is dedicated to the vulgar joy of building, from which architecture is born, and an oblique approach to learning, without which knowledge is impossible.

I hope that this bit of nonsense, sprinkled with fearful puns, double entendres, and the most shameless innuendos will aid the student in restoring some degree of rational perspective to this area of his education.

Forrest Wilson, Professor of Architecture
Athens, Ohio, 1974

INTRODUCTION

Survival Through Design

Once as evolution's fittest, the
brontosaurus stood victorious. He was
a mighty king. The earth shook when he
walked, and lesser creatures were
squashed beneath his notice. The
mighty dinosaurs looked down upon the
world and saw that it was good. "God
is a lizard," they croaked and worshipped a pantheon of lizard gods who
in their divine wisdom had created
reptiles first in the scale of evolution. But this mutation did not live
up to expectation and the great saurians
proved a bust as they sank beneath the
crust of the alluvial swamps.

Next came the mastodon. His pea-
shaped brain lodged between huge,
curved ivory tusks conceived god as
wooly elephant. But such colossal
piety did not influence the Pleistocene
deity, and the mastodon is long gone.

Then the gorilla in his ascendent
heyday worshipped god as a gleesome,
fleasome, prehensile marsupial. The
monkey was his reciprocal. The great
apes descended from their trees to
rule the earth. But today the
remnants of that mighty species wander
the fog-drenched forests on the moun-
tains of the moon, digging for grubs
among extinct volcanos. In sleep
the royal simians foul their nests as
they dream of their monkey god.

It is man's turn now, and he does
not lay the odds on lizard, mammoth, or
monkey gods. Man's faith is in his
divine survival through design.

PREHISTORIC ARCHITECTURE

The era of prehistoric architecture extended over countless millennia. Its beginnings are unknown, and its ending is undetermined. It has been said that man first began to build primitive buildings during the late Stone and early Bronze Ages, yet the construction of prehistoric buildings cannot be said to have terminated with the passing of these eras.

If the theory that we are the missing link between man and ape can be discounted, it can be assumed that we are subject to evolutionary change. However, it is doubtful that the brief ten thousand years that man has been known to inhabit the earth have been sufficient for the process of evolution to have had a measurable effect upon him. It may, therefore, be assumed that we exist in much the same primitive relation to architecture as did the builders of prehistory. It seems justified then to evaluate Stone Age architecture by

contemporary standards. Therefore, there is no mystery
in the meaning of prehistoric structures. The Stone
Ages have not been fully recorded since they have not
concluded. The most casual observation will substantiate the fact that politically adept Neanderthal man
still forges history from positions of eminence, and our
universities are stocked with some of the finest prehistoric minds.

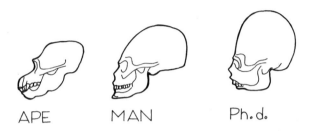

APE   MAN   Ph. d.

Man's first shelters were constructed of the trees
from which he descended. His initial decision to live
on the ground involved as traumatic a decision as the
contemporary family's move to the suburbs. Man constructed shelters from trunks and branches because he
felt the most comfortable monkeying around with familiar materials. This historic period coincided with
the dog's domestication, which rendered tree-constructed
dwellings damp and inhospitable. Man then occupied
caves since they had the virtue of prefabrication and
were devoid of canine kidney compulsion.

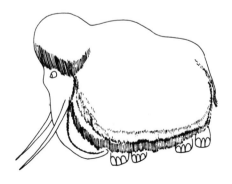

The cave possessed the psychological advantage of being admirably suited to prehistoric man's ideal of peaceful coexistence. This attitude can be summed up throughout the ages as a desire to integrate strangers, in a digested state, somewhere between his larynx and lower colon. The cave was thus rendered as desirable a dwelling place as the fallout shelter.

Cave decoration was confined to painting in the furthest recesses of the cave, prompted by the same sound logic of later architects who found that fine art is a remarkable antidote for awkward architectural spaces. The sculpture of the period was freestanding. It was confined to simple fertility figurines, very similar in proportion to the love goddesses of the contemporary screen, who, although similarly proportioned, bear them no conceivable resemblance.

Among the earliest of surviving monuments is that of Stonehenge in Wiltshire, England. The monument is made up of four concentric rings of huge stones, each weighing many tons. The structure was assuredly religious. The type of hoisting tackle then available would have been totally ineffective without the power of prayer. The outer ring of the monument is 106 feet in diameter and is comprised of thirty massive local stones tenoned at the head with dovetailed lintels. The ingenuity on the part of these early builders in employing the nether portions of feathered vertebrates as a means of stone joinery has never been equaled, even by modern mastics.

Civilization was reached when economic and social development had advanced sufficiently to allow the building of towns and cities. A proportion of the populace could thus engage in trade, industry, and professional pursuits. Among these we find contracts, subcontracts, mediation, and arbitration. These necessitated written records, which gave rise to more advanced indications of civilization. Copies of building contracts have been deciphered from the clay cuneiform-inscribed tablets of the Babylonians, and we find Hammurabi authoring the first building code.

Historic architecture, which followed while waxing and waning in virility, pursued a continuous evolutionary course—although occasionally waxing Roth in waning virility.

EGYPTIAN

$$\Sigma M = 0$$

$$M = \frac{WL}{8}$$

THE EGYPTIANS

The first notable development in architecture
occurred at the beginning of the third millenium
before Christ in the fertile valley of the Nile.
The Egyptians, who built the greatest monuments ever
constructed to the dead, evolved a culture that lived
longer than any to date.

Sandstone, limestone, and granite were employed
by Egyptian builders. The size of the monuments is
not only due to the skill of the Egyptian engineers
but also to the dexterity of quarrymen in removing
huge granite blocks from the quarries along the Nile.
The Egyptians used drilling and sawing as well as
wedges to cut their stone from the living rock. They
also employed dolerite balls for trenching harder
stones, a practice that resulted in the extinction of
the dolerite.

The great pyramid built by Khufu about 2800 B.C.
as his burial place is not only the most considerable
in bulk of any architectural work but one of the
most perfect in execution. Petrie reports, centuries
later, its divergence from exactness in equality of
sides, in squareness, and in level to be no greater
than his own probable error in measuring it with his
own instruments consisting of a rock tied to a string,
a length of garden hose filled with water, and a
level head.

The influence of religion on Egyptian architecture
is everywhere manifest. The priesthood was powerful,
it was invested with unlimited authority, and it was
sole possessor of the learning of the age, consisting
primarily of a body of dogma that affirmed the
divinity of the pharaoh. The mortality rate among
pharaohs equaled that of most mortals invested with
absolute power, surrounded by the luxuries of their
age, and subject to commandments of which they are
the sole arbiters. They all died young.

The religion was monotheistic in theory but polytheistic in practice. The many gods represented
natural phenomena, the heavenly bodies, the worship
of animals, the personification of deities, and,
since the religion was polytheistic, the deification
of parrots. The cat, introduced in Egypt as a counter-
measure against the mice and rats despoiling the royal
granaries, was deified in sculpture. However, its
architectural influence was limited to cathouses.

Memphite Period Or Old Kingdom

When the pharaoh Menes transferred the seat of government to Memphis, he took it with him. It was here that the great flowering of Egyptian art took place. The period lasted from the first to the tenth dynasties, 3200 to 2160 B.C.

The architectural form most frequently encountered in the old kingdom, the so-called mastaba, was commissioned by the Memphite nobles. It was a low, flat-topped mass, varying in size with the importance of the occupant. The solid bulk of early mastabas merely covered the rubble-filled shaft leading to the tomb chamber below. The design of a monument for a hole is a unique Egyptian contribution to the art of architecture.

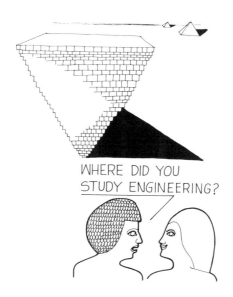

WHERE DID YOU STUDY ENGINEERING?

Mastabas declined in favor as pyramids became stylish. At the beginning of the Memphite dynasties the pharaohs adopted distinctive forms somewhat resembling later pyramids. The first king of the third dynasty, Zoser, built his tomb at Sakkara in seven great receding steps. The wisdom of receding steps was clearly understood by these ancient builders. If the steps had advanced, the pyramid would have been built upside down. King Snefru erected a similar pyramid of only three steps at Medum, since he did not have so far to travel.

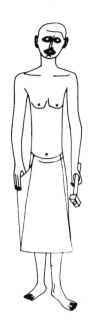

= CONTRACT

The most striking group of pyramids is that of the fourth-dynasty necropolis at Giseh. Here stands the familiar group of three, built by Khufu, Khafre and Menkure—the Cheops, Chepren, and Mycerinus of classic writers. Clustered around them are the smaller pyramids of royalty and the serried lines of mastabas. The interior arrangements differ, although there is little record of client criticism. They are alike in having the tomb chambers elaborately safe-guarded by granite portcullises and generalituses, the latter being a misleading passage.

Pyramids were preceded by massive chapels for religious services approached by causeways of stone leading up from the river—the only direction possible unless they had been constructed underwater. By their very size and simplicity of form these greatest of Egyptian monuments afford an unrivaled impression of grandeur and power. But when you have seen one pyramid, you have seen them all.

Rock-Cut Tombs

Under the Theban monarchies of the Middle Kingdom the characteristic forms of middle and upper Egyptian architecture were developed. Every wealthy Theban family had a concealed vault preceded by a small rock-cut chapel. To protect their mummies, the pharaohs built passageways, gradually descending and inter-rupted by small chambers for hundreds of feet into the cliffs. Their funerary chapels, however, became separated from the tombs themselves. They were erected on the plain before the cliffs fronting the river and in time became comparable to the temples of the gods on the opposite bank.

The first of such chapels, built by Queen Hatshep-
sut in the years from 1500 to 1480 B.C., is one of the
most original and refined of all Egyptian monuments.
It lies in the valley known as Deir-el-Bahri and rises
in three great colonnaded terraces to the rock-cut
sanctuaries. The architectural forms are the simplest
square or sixteen-sided columns arranged in long ranks.
The proportions are just and the effect so pure as to
suggest Greece in the days of Pericles. It was reported
that Sen-mut, the architect of Deir-el-Bahri, was a man
of genius, although there has been a tendency to dog
him down.

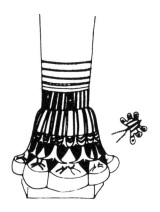

The Architect

During the whole of Egyptian history, the architect was a man of importance. This might be expected
when building formed so large a part of the monarch's
activity. Inscriptions in tombs of the fifth dynasty
show that in two cases at least the architect held
the combined functions of prime minister, chief jus-
tice, and royal architect roughly the equivalent of
the status of the architect as outlined in a contemporary architectural-design agreement.

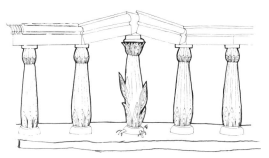

EGYPTIAN COLUMNS HAVE A DISTINCTIVE CHARACTER,
AND A VERY LARGE PROPORTION ADVERTISE THEIR
VEGETABLE ORIGIN,....

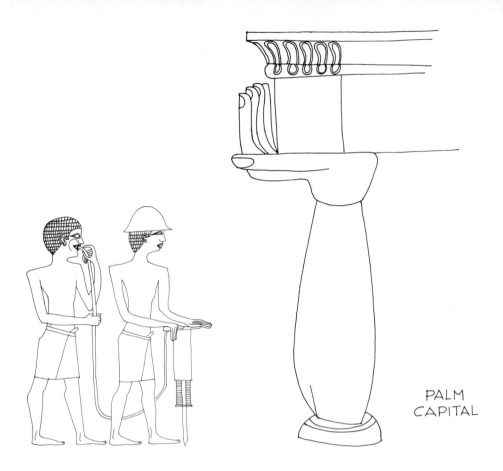

PALM
CAPITAL

Later Forms

Under the Middle Kingdom the most popular form
was a column, abstractly geometrical, polygonal in
plan, with concave vertical flutings. It was crowned
by a simple square abacus for calculating its dimensions. A capital with heads of the cow goddess,
Hathor, was used in her shrines. Piers fronted by
standing colossi were frequent, especially under the
great Ramessides. Sitting colossi were not as colossal,
especially under Ramessides.

The Peristyle

The interior peristyle was stylish, owing perhaps
to the guarded nature of Egyptian life and Egyptian
cults. A similar surrounding peristyle was rare,
exterior peristyles not being the style. A single
instance was the little temple of Elaphantine.

The Obelisk

Usually standing in pairs astride temple entrances were huge monoliths originating in the sacred symbol of the sun god Helippolis. They were square in plan and tapered to an electrum-capped pyramidion at the summit, which was the sacred part. The remainder was discarded after peeling.

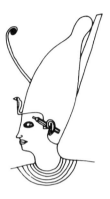

Dwellings

Ordinary dwellings were of crude brick. More cultured masonry meant working for the Assyrians. The houses were one or two stories high with flat or arched ceilings, depending upon the skill of the contractor. They had a parapet roof partly occupied by loggias (small female lodgers). Where space allowed, mansions stood in their own grounds, which were laid out formally with groves, gardens, pools, and minor structures surrounding them. These rectangular, crude, brick dwellings had doors and window openings dressed around with stone. The occupants dressed in the dark.

The earliest Egyptian buildings were constructed of mud and reeds. The weight of the roof-framing members at the top of the wall caused the wall section to bow out, a structural defect that was immortalized as a design feature by an alert architect in the famous Egyptian cove molding. While not remarkable in itself by contemporary standards, this is notable historically as the first instance where a client was persuaded that a structural miscalculation was in reality a design feature, leading to the contemporary dogma of total design through total error.

The last independent period of Egyptian history was ushered in by Alexander the Great, whose general, Ptolemy, conquered Egypt after his death. It lasted for three centuries and was an era of great prosperity with a continuation of the Egyptian religion and culture. The Ptolemaic Greek princess Cleopatra, who died of her aspirations, was the last Egyptian sovereign before Egypt became a Roman province.

THE ROMANS

The Romans were magnificent builders. Their soldiers thought it was camp to build themselves in for the night. Until 300 B.C., the Romans shared with the Etruscans a diluted Hellenism: that is, helling mingled with italic elements. From then until the end of the republic, about 250 years later, the Romans were absorbing from the western Greek colonies and from Greece itself the grammar of the orders, which they translated into fractured Latin.

The House

The most individual of this building type was
the dwelling. After the seventh century B.C. there
are few vestiges of houses. Except, of course, in
Pompeii, where vestiges vanished voluminously.

The Temple

There were two forms, the circular and the rectangular. The latter, with a single rectangular
cella, reproduced the typical Greek arrangement with
a few alterations. The portico in front was made
deeper, and the colonnade was frequently omitted at
the sides and always at the rear. The Greeks rued
rearing rear colonnades. The third form, with three
parallel cellas, may be looked on less as a structural
innovation than as part of the orchestration. Pro-
style cellas were placed side by side, which negated
the antistyle cellas and gave porticos somewhat more
depth—a logical outcome of this physical arrangement.

Arched Construction

Arches and vaulted drains, formerly thought to
descend from the bathrooms of legendary Roman kings
and to antedate Greek examples, are now placed at the
earliest in the fourth century B.C. They represent a
constructive advance but indicate a concerted effort
to give architectural expression to the functions.

The Architect

The Romans used captured slaves for architects rather than waste the time of their engineers on building decoration. These were usually captured among the Greeks. The Greeks were closest, and the Romans mistakenly thought that the Greek orders were a form of discipline. Architects were housed in slave pens, which explains the pensive nature of Roman architecture.

Columnar Systems

All three of the Greek orders find crude counterparts among the Romans. The Tuscan, thought to be the only original contribution of the Romans to the classic orders, was in reality the Greek Doric with the echinus reduced to a straight line and the quadrants rounded to a square without a base—a baseless molding of the Ionic order grown into the Corinthian. In this order the abacus did not figure; the echinus counted on the necking. The metope and triglyph were kept out of the bed molding, and a good thing! There were widely projected eaves, which formed the wooden beams and rafters and, like the architraves themselves, were cased in richly decorated terra-cotta or splashed with manicotti. A steep gable imitated the Greek pediment, sometimes with figure sculpture, or, if the budget was limited, sculpture was not figured. The impost and label molding opposed the impacted dentures. This avoided the impost becoming compost, no matter how heaped. The Romans employed both single and engaged columns, displaying no prejudice as to marital status. Less striking forms, such as dentils, put teeth into the composition.

By the middle of the second century B.C. most of the architects in Rome were Greek, and most architecture was Greek to the Romans. Henceforth, Greek standards need no longer be taken as criteria for Roman decoration. Roman membering was typified by the dismembering in the Coliseum.

There is, to be sure, always the conical subdivision of the entablature into architrave, frieze, and cornice. It was not until much later that the Turks, in the Greek wars of independence, proved their ability to cannonically subdivide the Greek orders in their bombardment of the Parthenon, which they did with a few well-directed salvos.

The Vault

The Romans developed the vault to enclose large areas and artfully placed an attic above the entablature to cover its structural appearance. Vaulting the attic was a high-stepping phase of Roman architecture.

Roman national life was administrative, commercial, pleasure loving, and egoistic. Beside luxurious palaces and temples for self-deification, the emperors erected triumphal columns to themselves and triumphal arches to their mistresses. It is not certain whether mausoleums were erected for moose, mass, mice, or Mies.

The adoption of Christianity in 330 A.D. caused the temples to fall into gradual disuse. Temples and public buildings alike were plundered for materials to build the great Christian basilicas. These were the only important undertaking of the period and were completed in time for the sack of Rome in 410 A.D. With the later sack of Rome by the Vandals in 455 A.D., the last vestiges of Roman imperial power became immaterial.

EARLY CHRISTIAN
ARCHITECTURE

Mediaeval

FINIAL

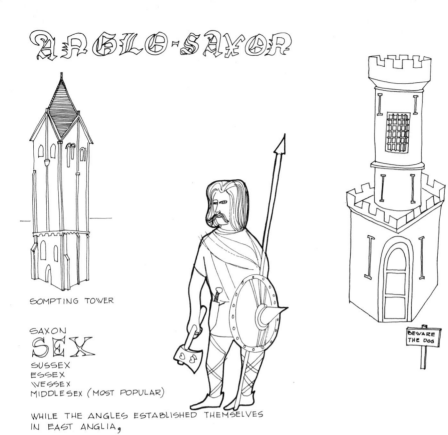

ANGLO-SAXON

SOMPTING TOWER

SAXON
SEX
SUSSEX
ESSEX
WESSEX
MIDDLESEX (MOST POPULAR)

WHILE THE ANGLES ESTABLISHED THEMSELVES
IN EAST ANGLIA,

BEWARE
THE DOG

The architecture that became known as early
Christian was in reality late Roman. The persecuted
became the persecutors, the meek became the most, the
temple became the martyr, the basilica became the
cathedral. The Huns and Vandals scrapped the lot.

The earliest of what is generally classed as the
medieval style thus had an appropriate beginning. It
is most often termed early Christian and Byzantine,
the former perhaps slightly antedating the latter.
This simple, clear classification often engenders a
profound confusion. One is apt to forget that the
latter is ipso facto early former. In short, the
two styles are roughly contemporary, frequently inter-
acting, and generally somewhat variegated manifesta-
tions of the same artistic movement, neophytes and
other pugilists notwithstanding.

The gestation of Christian art took place during
the Roman Empire's disintegration. In the decline of
the Roman Empire the canons of classical authority
lost their fire.

29

CASTLE HEDINGHAM ESSEX c. 1140

SCALLOP CAPITAL

IF THE ELEMENTARY BLOCK FORM OF THE CAPITAL IS GIVEN UP IT IS REPLACED BY FLUTING.....

NOW AT LAST THE VAULTING OF THE WIDER NAVES OF MAJOR CHURCHES WAS MASTERED —

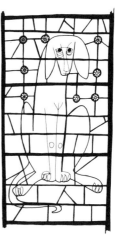

worms cathedral

THE GENERAL CHARACTER IS PICTURESQUE BY REASON OF NUMEROUS CIRCULAR AND OCTAGONAL TURRETS, POLYGONAL CUPOLAS ....

GENERAL CHARACTER

TURRETS

POLYGONAL

THE CHRISTIAN-ROMAN BASILICA

The Christian-Roman basilica had
a rudimentary transept with barely
civil salient sides. In front of the
building was a covered vestibule, or
narthex, and before that a peristylar
atrium open to the sky, with a font
in the center. Early Christians were
fond of founding fonts. The atrium
was for the unbaptized, for penitents,
and for pastenths. The apse, bema,
and often the upper nave were reserved
for the officiating clergy. This
space was enclosed by a railing, the
chancel, which frequently ran far down
into the nave. At the very back of
the apse, facing the congregation and
on the longitudinal axis, was the bis-
hop's chair, or cathedra; it was the
only place he could find a seat.

An interesting variation occurs
in the church of San Lorenzo in Rome.
Here, two churches, an early and a
later one, were oriented in opposite
directions and juxtaposed apse to apse
in an early form of bundling. Buildings constructed under the influence
of the facade and not the apse were
placed to face the east—eliminating
a possible face-to-face or traditional
cheek-to-cheek arrangement.

Between the clerestory windows
corbels often bore colonnettes after
a suitable period of gestation, which
ran up to receive the transverse
beams of the timber roof and gave the
structure a logical articulation amid
the patter of little feet.

S. Vitale - RAVENNA

COMPLETED 547 - BASICALLY IT IS AN
OCTAGON WITH AN OCTAGONAL
AMBULATORY

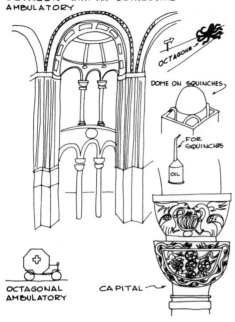

OCTAGONE

DOME ON SQUINCHES

FOR
SQUINCHES

OIL

OCTAGONAL
AMBULATORY

CAPITAL

THERE ARE IN ADDITION
A NARTHEX WITH
APSES AT BOTH
ENDS....

2 APSIS - AGED 2 TO 4

THE DESIGNER CLEARLY BELIEVED IN THE
EXPRESSIVE POSSIBILITIES OF CURVES....
HE SEPARATED THE CENTRAL OCTAGON
FROM THE AMBULATORY..... BY SEVEN
APSED SHAPES (THE EIGHTH IS THE CHANCEL)

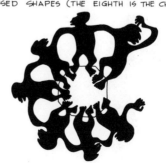

RENAISSANCE

RENAISSANCE ARCHITECTURE
WAS LESS CONCERNED WITH
PROBLEMS OF STRUCTURE...

Compared with the medieval architecture that preceded it, Renaissance architecture was less concerned with problems of structure and more with those of pure form. As in the case of Roman architecture, the forms of detail were sometimes used as trophies of classical culture with relative indifference to their original structural functions.

The forms were not merely ends in themselves, however, but means of thematic subdivisions of space, more complex and more varied than either ancient or medieval times had known.

A further contrast between the Middle Ages and
the Renaissance, though one which has often been
exaggerated, was in the relation of the designer
to his work. The architect, in the ancient and in
the modern sense, reappeared. The design was controlled by a single or singular mind. Unlike
medieval master builders, however, Renaissance
architects did not themselves work on scaffolds,
although in several instances they seemed to have
died on them.

The center of the new movement was Italy, where
the forces everywhere at work had their effect earlier
than in countries less richly endowed with the heri-
tage of antiquity. During the fourteenth and fif-
teenth centuries, Florence was the intellectual
capital of the peninsula, as well as one of the
greatest commercial powers in Europe.

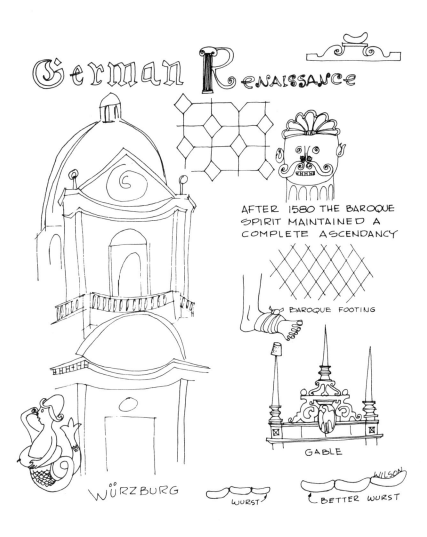

German Renaissance

AFTER 1580 THE BAROQUE
SPIRIT MAINTAINED A
COMPLETE ASCENDANCY

BAROQUE FOOTING

GABLE

WÜRZBURG

WURST

BETTER WURST

WILSON

EARLY RENAISSANCE
CORNICE
PIGEONS BY OTHERS

The soil of Italy was particularly favorable for a revival of the forms of classical architecture. The remains of ancient buildings existed on every hand in far greater completeness than they do today. They served, as they had since Constantine, as sources not only for stone and lime but also for the columns, entablatures, and archivolts that electrified the forms of later buildings. Thus, the feeling for classical architecture stole over Italy.

The early Renaissance dome of Brunelleschi involved no break with Florentine medieval tradition. Giving a steep curve to the dome enabled him to construct it, as Byzantine vaults had been constructed, without centering a self-centered dome. The whole was raised on a high drum to a regular beat and surmounted by a lantern to shed light on this structural accomplishment.

Maria degli Angeli is the first modern building to follow the mode of composition about a central axis later made popular by Mussolini.

A typical palace of the time is the Palazzo Medici, now Palazzo Riccardi, by Michelozzo. Its unbroken rusticated wall with windows in paired arches resting on colonnettes, the drum majorettes of classic times, are features of medieval derivation.

Thus, in the octagonal sacristy of Santo Spirito in Florence by Giuliano da Sangallo and Il Cronaca, a rhythmical grouping is introduced in a building of the centrally balanced type by an alternation of niches (small knishes) and shallow recesses of longer periods and shorter semicolons.

In his paganization of the church of San Francisco at Rimini, Alberti put great steak in the flank of a massive range of classic piers and arches. For the facade he used the triple motif of the Roman triumphal arch with engaged columns, their marital status was of the highest import to the church. He broke the entablature, but it was barely noticeable.

He also projected, as a termination for the building and to draw one's attention from the baroque entablature, a circular, domed room of the proportions of the Pantheon, a form which he later emphasized in the church of the Annunziate in Florence, although there the entablature remained intact.

His Palazzo Pitti was a range of vast rusticated arches reminiscent of the Roman aqueducts, although in this instance the design does not hold water. Another time-honored scheme that Alberti revived was the Greek-cross plan with four equal arms in the church of San Sebastino at Mantua (which was later double-crossed by Sant'Andrea), begun in 1470. Here, he again made use of the triumphal arch for the double cross, not only in the porch but on the interior walls, continuing to act as a nave.

For the first time in a Renaissance church the nave itself was vaulted in a classical manner with long poles, the first indication of sport in architecture. It also features the unbroken, coffered break of a barrel vault.

Alberti's influence included some of the most literal reproductions of the antique yet attempted. The great range of superposed porticos successfully imitated Roman examples in proportions, although their success might be questioned due to the continued breaking of entablatures and pedestals at each engaged column.

Alberti's ideas were further developed by Luciano the unlucky Laurana, architect of the ducal palace at Urbino. In a series of imaginary compositions he suggested a circular temple and gave the models for most of the schemes later used in palace design by his two great followers, at a distance, Bramante and Raphael.

In the Palazzo Cancelleria in Rome continuous alternation of wide and narrow spaces between the pilasters, the rhythmical bay, reminiscent of fox hounds, which Alberti had used in an interior, was employed. Terminal masses of slight projection, end pavilions of dubious and perhaps pornographic connotation, appear for the first time.

Elsewhere, except for isolated works of the Florentine and Roman schools, the new forms were adopted only gradually; seldom were they born legitimately.

Inspired by the works of Alberti and Laurana, Donato Bramante took up the main thread of development. In the sacristy of Santa Maria in San Satiro in Milan and other churches, he made important contributions to local officials, which assured him the contracts. He solved the problem of buildings composed about a central axis. At Abbiate Grasso, he prefixed to the church a great arched porch, recalling an ancient exedra and so forth. It was supported on pilasters, which here, almost for the first time, were coupled or grouped in pairs. It is not recorded that they were engaged.

Venice scarcely took up the new forms before 1470, when the family of architects called Lombardi began their work there. In general, their style is a translation of the local Byzantine and Gothic motifs into pseudoclassic forms, carried out with rich marble incrustation in place of the usual barnacles. The Palazzo Vendramini is perhaps its best representative. As in the Palazzo Rucellai the facade is decorated with superposed orders, or posures.

On the other hand the arches are subdivided by tracery that is essentially medieval to spite its classic details. As usual in Venice, the retention of a threefold subdivision of the width results in a complicated rhythmical grouping of the supports, many of which were athletic.

The second, mature period of the Renaissance, the High Renaissance as it is sometimes termed, began at Rome with the papacy of Julius, or High Julius. The lavish court and great undertakings—the mortuary business thrived—attracted to the city the finest talent of all Italy, including Bramante, Raphael, Leonardo da Vinci, and Michelangelo.

Bramante was the moving spirit in the new Roman
school of architecture. In the shrine at the place of
Saint Peter's martyrdom, Bramante outvied all his pre-
decessors in classical ardor. The ardorous Bramante
constructed a Roman circular temple with its peristyle, the so-called Tempietto, or "small trombone,"
church. It is surmounted by a dome on a tall drum,
which was somewhat base and was intended to be surrounded by a circular, colonnaded court.

On Bramante's death in 1514, Raphael succeeded to
the architectural directorship, keeping it afloat. He
executed the loggias at the Court of San Damaso, which
was not very nice but no worse than smothering the
small princes in the Tower of London. He revived the
stuccoed decorations of the Roman interiors in a moment of contrition. Thus arose the graceful compositions of leafage, figures, and small medallions
(medium-sized horses), as architecture raced toward
the twentieth century.

MODERN ARCHITECTURE

From the pillar to post-Renaissance, architecture adopted a series of successive seasonal passions. It got itself entangled with the eclectic and the eclectac, with romantic revivalism and prosaic survivalism, art nouveau and art must go, funk and functionalism, the Bauhaus, the doghouse, and the service station.

Architecture became everything and nothing. It expanded to include the "entire environment" defined by Buckminster Fuller as everything outside oneself, which meant that we could all forget about it. But no matter what anyone said, everybody continues to do it; we have more architecture every day and know less and less about it.

The architecture of the past consisted mostly of important individual buildings in their natural or quaint village settings. This world of historic architecture has disappeared and in its place we have a totally man-made environment. Design is everywhere. Everything around us has been designed by some group or some person. The only undesigned things urban people ever see are broken pavements, wrecked automobiles, and garbage piles. Design is escaped only by accident.

Now the emphasis of this book must change. Architecture on such an all-encompassing scale is no longer an activity that can be laughed off with puns and double-talk. The following short essays are therefore submitted to serious students of the environment to aid them in comprehending that which, without this explanation, might continue to be incomprehensible.

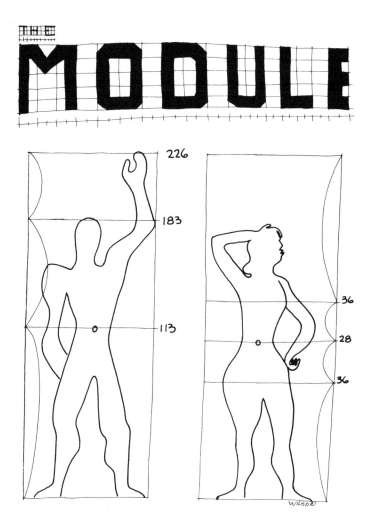

MODULE

THE NODULE ON THE MODULE

More than any other single architectural concept, the module represents man's age-old reaction to the immeasurable chaos that surrounds him. In supplying rational dimensions, it satisfies his atavistic urge for order. The history of the module may be divided into four distinct periods: the archaic, the classic, the fluorescent, and the surfeit—in human terms, the ages of Pythagoras, Leonardo, Le Corbusier, and the punch press.

Probably the first attempt to fabricate a measured system was the sun-dried brick. That prehistoric module was manufactured to the practical formula of the size of an Assyrian bricklayer's hand times the temper of his foreman divided by the effectiveness of his union delegate. A module of convenience, it produced few buildings worthy of publication, and it remained for the designer to metamorphose the principle of harmonious proportion into the modular system.

While it is comparatively simple to produce an unlimited quantity of bricks from the same mold, the manufacture of a man involves a decidedly different set of principles. The problem of creating a harmonious structure, dimensionally controlled, to shelter people who are dimensionally unstable is the essence of the designer's problem and the basic contradiction inherent in module theory.

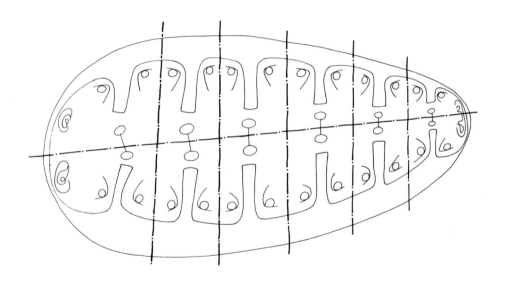

During the archaic modular period, the Greeks, led by Phythagoras, evolved the golden section to solve half the dilemma. The golden section is a harmonious sytem of related measurements; but they left it at that, abandoning man to adjust himself to the harmonies of their structures as best he might. It was not until the Renaissance, when man was adjudged the measure of all things, that Leonardo decided to measure man.

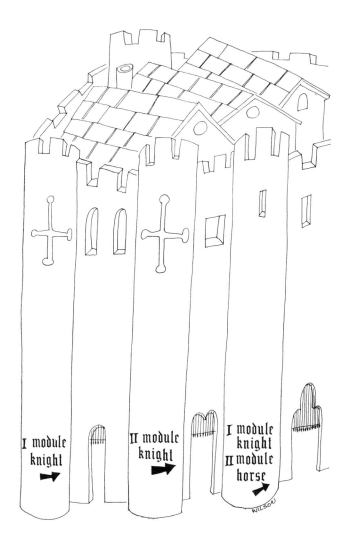

I module
knight
➤

II module
knight
➤

I module
knight
II module
horse
➤

WILSON

Leonardo da Vinci ushered in the classic modular period by placing his ideal man in an ideal square and using the ideal man's navel as a center scribed in a run-of-the-mill circle. The truly well-proportioned man standing in the square with his arms extended brushed his ideal fingertips against the run-of-the-mill circumference.

While this represented a logical and intelligent measuring system, it obviously depended upon the ideal navel being dimensionally stable. It was undoubtedly a lopsided navel, creating an ellipse, that spelled the doom of the Renaissance and the birth of the baroque.

Modern architecture ushered in the fluorescence of the module. Le Corbusier sought and invented a modular system of measurement that would instill harmonious proportion in the manufactured component. For the basis of this sytem, Le Corbusier placed a man within two juxtaposed, congruent squares, the common side positioning a horizontal line through the man's navel. He then predicated a series of golden sections upon the height of a six-foot Englishman (his early calculations involving a 175-centimeter Frenchman produced irrational numbers). During the fluorescent period, now past, we again observe the navel as the center of pertinent calculation.

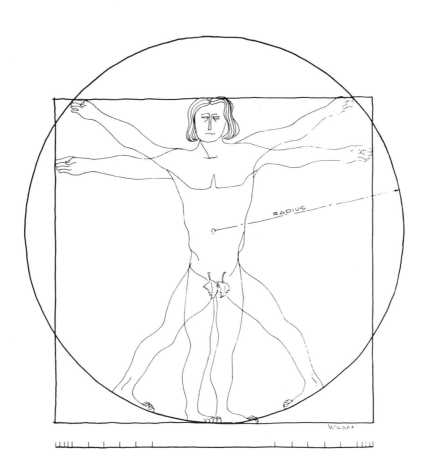

Leonardo da Vinci's
IDEAL MAN

While the position of man's navel resulted in the
golden period of the module, furnishing the concept of
a basis of building sizes related to the harmonious
proportions of man and fixing comfortable heights for
knees, pelvis, head, and elbows, the navel itself does
not seem to possess architectural pertinence. Its
existence seems merely a nodule on the module.

From the foregoing it may be concluded that man
has found success in developing harmonious proportions when he based his calculations on the scar left
by the termination of the umbilical cord. The uncon-
testably satisfactory results and the irrefutable
logic of such a process binds us to examine the present period, the surfeit age of the module, in the
light of this scientific discovery.

Such an examination will disclose that we have
again slipped back to chaos through the very means we
used to escape it. Our urban landscape is dominated
by the machine module in the greatest profusion of
confusion. We have lost the harmonious module of
man to the haphazard module of the machine, indicating
that either man's navel has moved or other navels are
being calibrated.

Casual observation of a Turkish dancer in repose
will reassure the observer that belly buttons are as
charmingly placed as ever. If we are going to remain
firm in our rejection of the human dimension, perhaps
we should, in this mechanized world, search for and
locate the navel of the machine. We could then proceed
to predicate a system of golden sections upon this new
reference point and once again begin to transform chaos
into ordered, harmonious environment—if not for man,
at least for the machine.

THE ART OF WAR

All the arts through their divine origin bear resemblance, but the art of war is unique among the
Muses, for it alone contains a principle that can be
mathematically determined and contained within an
elementary algebraic formula: the artistic labor
expended upon military adornment stands in inverse
proportion to the ease of human extermination.

Prehistoric man decorated his body profusely and
did battle in single combat. Technological necessity
coupled with an instinctively refined sensibility re-
stricted him to the simplest of weapons. The body of
his adversary, tatooed since puberty, demanded a certain delicacy in the alteration of its configurations.
Such a challenge was a stimulation to early man's aesthetic impulses.

The independent variable in man's restless search
for eternal beauty is constant change. Personal decoration soon moved from the body itself to its covering.
Slaves were employed to emboss shields, hone javelins,
and true arrow shafts. This early form of specializa-
tion cheapened the cost of decoration and, by leaving
the warrior free to find reason to use his weapons,
accelerated the pace of killing. The need for delicacy
was also removed, since it was not possible to smash
an opponent's head without causing damage to his surface decor.

At this point the Muses once again inspired the creation of improved weaponry, heralding another destructive advance at further cost to design integrity. The cultural achievement of the crossbow decimated the adherents of the old art forms, ushering in an age of deep-rooted Christian faith that required for survival the encasing of the entire body in embossed steel.

The decorative aspect of the art of war of this new age was created by countless metalsmiths, who covered every joint of the knightly body and every tendon of his noble horse with finely engraved steel. The virtuous knight then did battle in bloody combat peering through slits in his artwork. He was accompanied into battle by his faithful smithies clad in leather jerkins. The art of war proceeded at a comfortable ratio, with the destruction of 12,362 smiths for the denting of one major metal magnum opus.

Such a state of affairs might have continued unchanged and unlamented by those in charge of changes had it not been for the introduction of gunpowder. This did to the art of war what Pollock, at a later date, did to the art of painting. Gunpowder caused irreparable damage to the engraved carapaces and their contents and ushered in a new medium of personal adornment. Specialized metal embossing and its attendant warring at a leisurely pace were replaced by the needle and thread and the beginning of serious slaughter.

Now, brightly colored weavings and bits of gold braid introduced a chromatic improvement over the leather jerkin, increasing the pride, vulnerability, and visibility of the soldier. For those who found even this target difficult, soldiers were arranged in orderly lines and fitted with tall bearskin hats to facilitate the setting of sights.

During the formative period of the age of cloth, the muzzle-loader had proven sufficiently effective, but it was soon discarded for the more efficient breech-loading device tipped by a decorative bayonet. As the art of war proceeded in its killing pace, color was reduced to bits of braiding with the addition of a cunning steel helmet carrying a sensitively designed spike on its crown.

As the slaughter became more efficient, expressionist coloration was replaced by a dominant monochrome. Man, who had formerly been the prime objective of the decorative treatment, had become so easily exterminated that more important objects were embellished. Gun emplacements, airplanes, battleships, and zeppelins were all subjected to cubist surface treatment. This development gave rise to the myth of the invincible marksmanship of the German underwater navy. The First World War (and later tests) proved conclusively that on a blue ocean it was impossible for even the most poorly aimed torpedo to miss a floating Picasso.

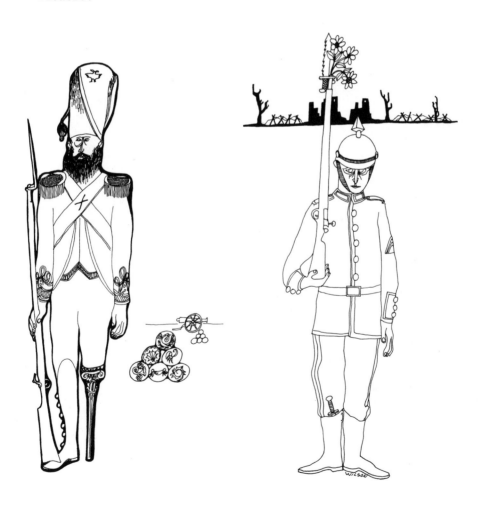

With the passing of cubism and the arrival of the second global conflict, the art of war advanced to the postcubist forms, exhibiting a marked preference for those of Miro, upon which Adolph Hitler died of pique at seeing the work of a painter he had banished as decadent returning to a toilet-trained Germany.

Five years later an exhibition of minor importance took place in a Korean gallery but did not establish any new trends, excepting that Pollock set the camouflage motif. It added little else to military adornment and contented itself with the comparatively classic forms of slaughter.

Today, as we stand on the verge of the third and final world exhibition, an examination of our original formula allows a prediction of the final canvas. That formula, establishing the inverse ratio of decoration to destruction, need only have the necessary terms inserted. Pop art has destroyed decoration as the hydrogen bomb can destroy everything else, thus furnishing the two requisite zeros for each side of the equation and proving its validity. The third and final global exhibition may therefore be drawn upon a radioactive landscape with contestants clad in Campbell-soup cans and Brillo boxes.

RICHARD THE LIONHEARTED ARCHITECT, AS A KNIGHT OF THE GARTER

By definition, a metaphor is literal rather than architectural; however, it is most fittingly adapted to the mother of the arts, since she has been under the domination of literature since Vitruvius.

Let us first clarify what a metaphor is. It is an intuitive truth proven by an illogical example.

We might, for illustration, analyze the oft-quoted epithet, Richard the Lionhearted. Here, we obviously do not mean that Richard had a lion's heart. If he had, his coronary condition would have prevented his wielding any weapon more deadly than a penknife. The metaphor is used to poetically characterize and romanticize the fearlessness of Richard. Clinically, Richard was a psychopathic nut.

As one might expect of a profession dominated by literary values, metaphors are an integral part of the practice of architecture. Yet, the metaphor is not part of the architect-client contract. No value has been assigned to it; it is the priceless commodity that the client gets for nothing. But if he did not expect this extra metaphorical service, he would engage a builder or engineer in place of the architect.

Under most circumstances the architect can indeed be compared to Richard the Lionhearted as he mounts his charger and sets out in quest of the holy metaphor on a budget that would not buy enough hay to fuel his horse from here to Canarsie.

However laudable our truehearted knight's commitment to upholding metaphoric truth and beauty, style and fashion against the dragon, he is obviously predestined for defeat. Our knight-errant architect is outgunned, outclassed, and surrounded before he unsheathes his 6B pencil.

The corporate client will pay a public-relations consul or advertising advisor many times over what he will pay his architect to create metaphors. This, of course, may be justified in the metaphor market. How can the architect compete with metaphors that make automobiles animals, have lung cancer riding on a horse in Marlboro country, and deodorize intercourse? What can rival the triumphant, rampant metaphor, which is in reality that subtle distinction between seduction and rape known as salesmanship?

The dragon that the Lionhearted Richard must slay is the dilemma of the architect, a dilemma posed by the present quiet metaphor of architecture on the one hand and the realization of the heights that architectural design might aspire to were it freed to compete in the open market. What if architecture were, in reality, able to create planned-obsolescent metaphors in commercial competition? What if the architect were freed from the ever-present worry of his metaphors lasting long enough to become cliches?

The wisdom of adopting the commercial metaphor is obvious. The mystery is why architects have not seem that this was the only workable solution to the dilemma of a society that has generated problems too complex to solve realistically.

As a beginning, architects might consider selling metaphors that they usually give away. If the architect accepts the opportunities of a free-enterprise society, the architectural metaphor might be marketed competitively with breakfast cereals and detergents.

A PROPOSAL

The following modest proposal will put the roar back into the heart of Richard, our architectural lion. It might be entitled, "Measure for Measure; or, Architectural Foundations in the Age of Exhibitionism."

Throughout the ages architects have sought metaphoric correspondence between human proportions and building dimensions as the touchstone of design. It was called "symmetry" by Vitruvius, "harmony" by Alberti, and the "Modulor" by Le Corbusier.

We have today a ready-made means of upgrading the metaphor to make it viable in the competitive commercial market. If architects would adopt, in place of the ideal man, a well-endowed pantyhosed maiden inscribed in the classic Vitruvian square and circle, the problem would be solved.

This is not an original idea. The creators of metaphors for lingerie have already adopted the idea of mother of the arts turned flapper. On the other hand, in all fairness, architectural criticism has in many instances used the language of lingerie advertising.

To substantiate these claims I would like to compare a few quotations: "Without symmetry and proportion there can be no principle in design," wrote the Roman architect Vitruvius, "as in the case of a well-shaped man. It was by employing symmetry that the famous painters and sculptors of antiquity attained to endless reknown."

During the Renaissance, Alberti described the perfect form for a church as "organic geometrical equilibrium where all parts are harmonically related, like the human body". A little later, Vasari amplified the grand design to include a plumbing layout. "An ideal palace," he wrote, "must represent the human body of a man in the whole and similarity of the parts; and as it has to fear wind, water, and other natural forces, it should be drained by sewers."

During the Middle Ages, as we all know, the cathedrals represented the outstretched body of a man; the transepts, his extended arms; and the apse, his head. Villard de Hardencourt left his designs for steeple and pinnacle, based on the star formed by a human face.

Just as the metaphor of the human body has been an
architectural inspiration, so it has inspired today's
lingerie-advertising copy. For example, the following
aesthetic statement appeared in a well-known woman's
magazine: "Your tummy's in line with your hips, your
hips aren't too round for your thighs and your derriere.
You get as nearly perfect a shape as you can have, not
just a plain body! Our bras and girdles proportion you
so every part of your body goes with every other part."

In another magazine we found this advice, "Chances
are that you have never been fitted properly from waist
to crotch—that's the secret, waist to crotch—the only
accurate way. Artful control panels persuade tummy,
thighs, and fanny to behave."

Note the similarity of the following comments gleaned from the remarks of a prestigious architectural jury: "The simplest, clearest, and most controlled use of an idiom that seems to be everywhere . . . we're not judging this as a house but as the ability of someone to manipulate a few forms and a few surfaces; it just happens to be a house . . . This form is only attainable by having two of them . . . You've got to fill in all of those wonderful voids with something that keeps the winter out."

The stretch-bra architectural-metaphorical system
has been in operation for some time, although it is
still ignored in architectural criticism. For instance
what better metaphor for the Seagram Building than
Twiggy, compared to the monumental, uplifting architecture of Marcel Breuer in his Whitney Museum. And
Edward Durell Stone's concrete filigrees perform functions of enticement similar to lacy underwear by afford-
ing the same tantalizing glimpses of unseen structures.

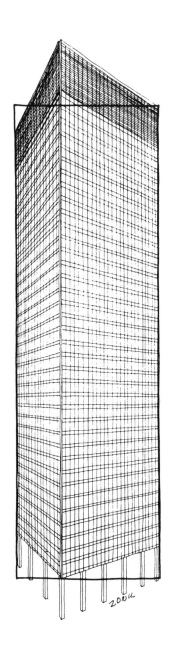 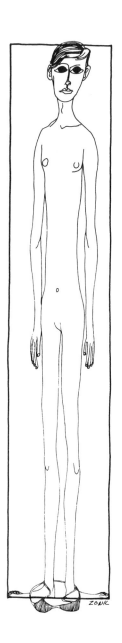

    Metaphoric principles of the ladies-undergarment
industry tend to keep architecture abreast of the times
by putting architecture into the shape the rest of the
society is in. This natural evolution of metaphors is
characteristic of all great ages of architecture.

    Let us conclude by saying that we firmly believe
the future belongs to the Miss Fit. She symbolizes a
true metaphoric mother of the arts that knights of the
garter can defend and not come away empty-handed.

SOME MODEST PROPOSALS FOR THE REDESIGN OF MAN

My God, The Transit Mix

"In the beginning God created the heavens and the earth; the earth was waste and void . . . God said, 'Let there be light,' . . . And so it was . . . God said 'Let the dry land appear'. And so it was, and God saw that it was good. Then God said, 'Let the good earth bring forth vegetation, seed-bearing plants, and all kinds of fruit trees that bear fruit containing their seed.' God saw that it was good . . . God said 'Let us make mankind in our image and likeness.' God created man in his image; in the image of God he created him."—Then man created the bulldozer and reversed the entire process.

If man was made in God's image, as quoted in Genesis, it is logical to assume that man, in reversing the process of creation, is doing so in man's image. Deductively, we may, therefore, assume that things equal to the same thing are equal to each other, and conclude that God is the bulldozer, or, as the Greeks and Romans so aptly put it, <u>deus ex machina</u>.

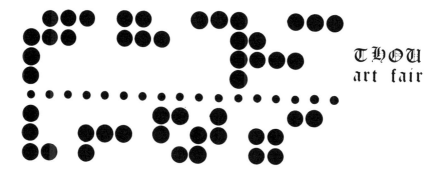

𝔗𝔥𝔬𝔲
art fair

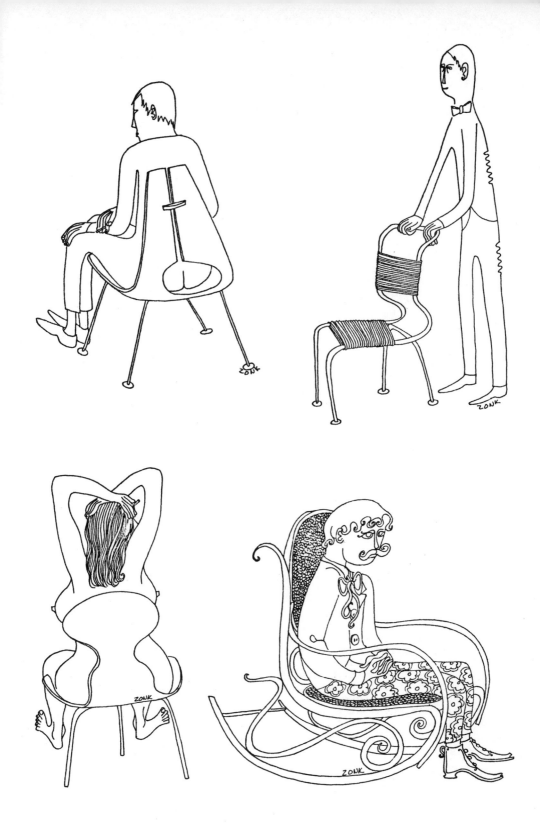

From the weakest (when the dinosaur was top lizard,
man was a shrew), from the slowest (the saber-toothed
tiger made a monkey out of man), from the not overly
bright (it cannot be demonstrated that man is not dumb-
er than the dolphin), man became the king of beasts.
So how—if not so strong and not so fast and not so
smart—did man emerge as prime primate of the vertebrates? His magic ingredient has always been his
ability, through malleability, to maintain his plausibility.

From a cool fish that found there was no wave of
the future to a smart monkey that decided progress was
not entailed, man adapted as the surroundings demanded.
Survival of the fittest has always been the game at
which he was the most proficient. As man the malleable, his docile ductility has stretched and bent as
other evolutionary contenders came and went.

However, at this moment of evolutionary triumph,
man faces the major crisis of his evolutionary career.
For in his emergence as top evolutionary dog, he finds
that his highest human achievement has been to create
an inhuman environment. In holding the mirror up to
nature he perceives a bulldozer. Man is stunned and
alienated by the enormity of his accomplishment. For
the first time in his evolutionary history his progress has halted, not by adversity but by success.
There is nothing that recedes like success.

Man must be reactivated at all costs before he
begins to tread the environmental lane of lonely
evolutionary losers like the loris. He must once
again become the adjustee rather than the adjuster.
It must be admitted man has created an environment
most difficult to adapt to. However, following are
some modest proposals for the redesign of contemporary man, dedicated to his survival. These suggestions,
if heeded, might restore man once again to his position of prime primate of the vertebrates instead of
an evolutionary castrate.

Contaminated Man

As air changes from an invisible, tasteless mixture
of gasses to blinding, choking fumes, as the sea mother
becomes the repository of atomic wastes and the land is
sown with bent metal that, unlike offal, will not sink
back into the earth to contribute its cells to new life,
it remains to be seen if man can triumph in the re-
shuffling of the basic elements, air, earth, and water.

It is unfortunate that man must cope with pollution
this late in his environmental development. If as a fish
he had been forced to imbibe petroleum wastes, he might
today be able to drink gasoline and gain pleasure and
sustenance from sniffing automobile mufflers. Since this
is not the case, he will have to adjust as best he can or
relinquish his primacy.

Other species have succeeded in adapting. There has
been a report by ornithologists that a gradual change in
bird life is taking place. Industrial fumes tend to
fuse the birds' feathers together into plastic-like coat-
ings that improve their waterproofing qualities but unfortunately make them useless for pillows. Bird droppings are gradually approaching the neat merchandising
characteristic of the rabbit and the deer, with the
addition of plastic coating. This development has been
applauded by sextons, sculptors, and ferryboat passen-
gers. It has also been reported by sportsmen that the
flesh of game brids is beginning to taste of smog.

The ocean's creatures have not been unaffected by
the dumping of radioactive wastes in the sea. Fish
droppings have become explosive. An angler off the
Jersey shore is reported to have lost his first and
second digits through a small atomic explosion attri-
butable to an uninhibited halibut.

A change in salamander physiology in the Jersey
flats has been reported. These creatures, heretofore
unnoticed and the sole living survivors of mass contamination of the marches, have thrived in contaminated
earth, polluted water, and noxious fumes for almost a
century.

There have been reports from a major coke plant that salamanders have eaten completely through a six-inch cast-iron soil line in search of food. And their ability to live in fire, long considered a medieval superstition, is apparently fact, not fiction. These wet lizards, living in the reducing furnaces, have been known to consume live coals, instead of the coals consuming them. They gnaw steel rivets of the plant construction and are generally becoming a nuisance, although they are not unfriendly.

At this time, laboratory experiments have been confined to simply observing the salamander, since no known dissecting instrument, including the band saw, has any effect upon their contaminated hides. It is extremely unfortunate that this breed of salamander remains benign, for it is doubtful that man could compete with these creatures who have enjoyed a head start in evolutionary contamination. We must follow the examples of the bird, the fish, and the salamander to survive. This means exposure to contamination and air pollution as early and regularly as possible. The feasibility of piping fumes to the womb should be carefully probed.

However, man, in cloaking cities in fumes, polluting entire rivers, and fouling hundreds of square miles of earth, is creating the total contaminated environment. Man can be expected to rival the salamander in evolution, as soon as he gets a sufficient whiff of what is going on.

Modular Man

We have architecturally solved the problems of
the module. The module now functions magnificently,
aside from the minor problem of major human discom-
fort. We have modulated man to high-rise honeycombs,
cellularized his every waking function, and compart-
mentalized his wants to the binary demands of the
computer. However, in our haste, we have overlooked
the fact that he does not produce modulated wigglers.

To be or not to be is no longer the question.
The module demands that man be a bee. The evolutionary solution is obvious. Man must himself become modular by the de-evolutionary stratagem of
mating with the insect. The benefits are obvious.
It will incude a natural, modular, cellular, structural proclivity and at the same time further man's
survival potential as the eventual inheritor of a
radioactive earth. Such a union will dimension man,
who heretofore has been the measure of all things,
to the regulated portion of a grub.

The moral implication is obvious. Man's indecent
haste to reduce his varied world to the simplicity of
insect necessity could only be motivated by ants in
his pants.

Titillating Evolution

In weaning the young from the breast to the bottle, man has accomplished, during the ten thousand years he has been known to inhabit the earth, the single evolutionary change in his physiology.

When the breast fell out of use as a tastefully designed food container, it did not degenerate to the status of the vermiform appendix but instead developed other uses. It provides a well-placed bumping apparatus in a region unrestrained by seat belts and, in addition, may function as a built-in barbell, allowing the individual to keep physically fit by merely tying her shoes.

Scientists have been watching the development closely and report that they feel there may be an auxiliary breathing apparatus, or smog filter, developing naturally in the mammary area.

Hollywood, in its usual opportunistic exploitation of the sensational under the justification of "feeding the public what it wants" has anachronistically exploited the breast as a sex symbol. Nothing could be further from the truth. Children suckled on glass and tin containers tend to transfer their affections to neoprene gaskets and milk containers. This was dramatically demonstrated recently when a young man with a severe Oedipus complex tried unsuccessfully to marry a can of condensed milk.

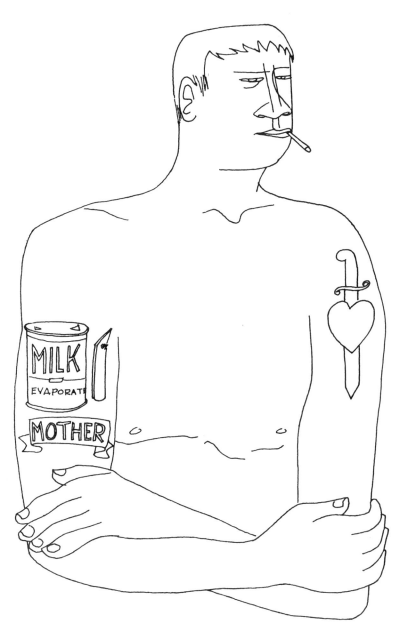

Plastic, Or Silly Putty, Man

Life in the water was compressed to the form of a
fish; in the trees, to the limbs of a monkey; and in
the cave, molded to the form of a man. Today, the
former caveman is molten rather than molded by glass
and steel, with no indication of the new growth to
sprout from the influence of his synthetic environment.

Instead of bending steel and glass to his lumpy
irregularities, he should be researching the possibilities inherent in modern chemicals and plastics of
making himself more ductile, malleable, elastic, and
durable. His ideal viscosity should be completely
plastic, or roughly the consistency of silly putty.

Such a condition, by its very nature, would neces-
sarily discard the distortion-eliminating device of the
backbone. Man, if properly compounded, might be seen
through both literally and figuratively. A dependable
man—in short, the ideal projected by the advertising
media.

Man, thus deprived of all vestiges of rigidity
in his system, could reproduce, when passion dictated,
like the amoeba, by twisting himself into segments.
Not only would this free him from a ridiculous position
and damnable expense for momentary pleasure, but, in
a glass building, would seem the only decent thing to
do.

Plastic man would be incapable of being cornered
or permanently creased. He would flow around his
perforations and mutilations. He would be the ideal
man of our time, maintaining his plausibility through
malleability—silly putty in the hands of his environment.

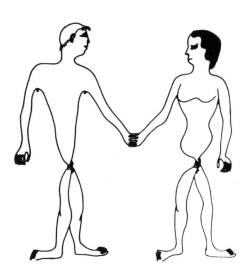

UGLINESS MAKES AMERICA GREAT

There are many words for ugliness and every one of them can be found in descriptions of our built environment. Yet ugliness is an arbitrary term. Strip-mined hillsides, fouled rivers, corrosive air are the physical results of man's conversion of nature's raw materials to consumer goods. Nature herself is guilty of occasional ugly acts, such as hurricanes and earthquakes, but she does not consistently create ugliness. That takes human intelligence; you have to be smart to be ugly.

The deteriorating quality of the environment is often attributed to a general diminishing of popular aesthetic sensibilities. The facts are otherwise. It can be shown that public participation and appreciation of the arts has increased in direct proportion to the growth of the gross national product. Never before in our history have so many people paid to enter museums and bought tickets to concerts and the theater.

Fouled rivers, smoky air, and
mine tailings are the marks of a
progress universally welcomed by
the peasants of poor nations around
the world. An untouched country-
side, clean air, and clear water
are certain indications of a poor
nation that cannot afford symphony
orchestras, art galleries, monumental architecture, disposal tis-
sues, or no-deposit beer bottles.

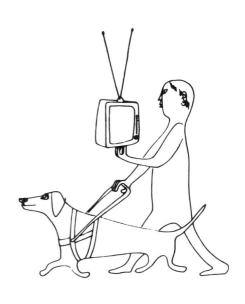

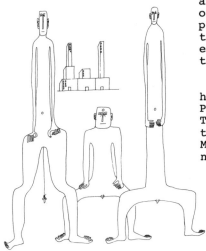

Environmental ugliness is a direct measure of culture. Good design and good taste are financed and supported by a system capable of providing wealth that cannot be produced without environmental contamination. We cannot deny the equation of production equals pollution.

God's own junkyard could only have occurred in an affluent society. Poor people have nothing to discard. There is no litter to be found on the backcountry roads of Africa, Mexico, or South America. Cleanliness is next to poverty.

ZONING

Although the cultured are the most likely to condemn the pollution of nature and extol the virtues of natural conservation, culture itself cannot be linked to virtue. We can thank the anthropologists for demonstrating that the slave-owning tribes of Africa were always more cultured than the tribes they enslaved. Culture demands excessive production.

It is possible that art and architecture can thrive without affluence. There could conceivably be an architecture that promoted a benign rather than a destructive use of the environment. There could even be an architecture that promoted a good fit, physically and perceptually, between man and his environment. But this would not be architecture or art as we know them, but something else.

The aesthetic, political, and economic rules that define contemporary architecture, the schools that train its practitioners, and the press that accords them recognition would all have to change the rules of the game.

A game is defined by its rules, which include the players, what they can do, their value systems, and the available alternatives and payoffs. It is possible to change these rules, but once this is done, a different game has been created.

The rules that govern architecture have been formulated by the architectural profession, its clients, the political and economic climate, and a philosophy dependent upon affluence for its aesthetics.

Our concept of architecture is preserved by these rules, for they reinforce and give art and architecture its identity. An attack against the economic base, a threat to affluence, a plea for social and economic readjustment, a denigration of the political justifications that create affluence is in reality an attack against culture and against art and architecture as we know them. Ugliness makes America great.

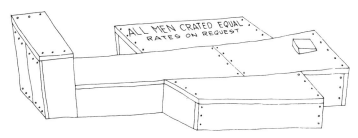

PERSUIT OF HAPPINESS
ATHLETIC SUPPLIES

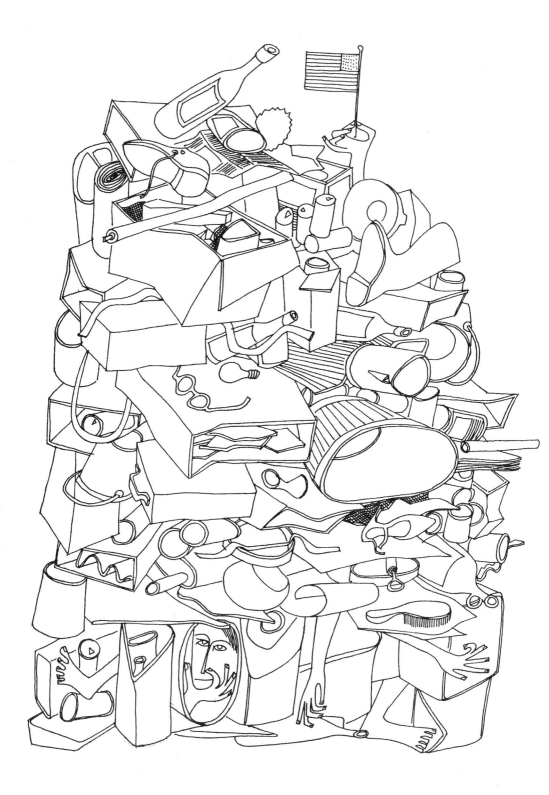